I Look @ your fa
for what you ha

when you read th
Keep In mind That we never
Wanted was a family like your's

God has a plan, one for all & its
Such a blessing to be a witness
to the beautiful plan God has for
you guys.
        Lots of Love!!
            xxx

GUTTER TO GLORY
God is Soooo, GooD! 🖤
    by

Kerri Douglas

DEDICATIONS

There are so many people that I have to thank in this life. People that have brought me to where I am today, So, I'm really sorry if I miss you out, you all hold a place in my heart.

Firstly, I want to thank the dream team Kath, Leah and Lucy without you ladies encouraging me and loving me through, some of the hardest moments of my recovery, my life would not be what it is today.

Secondly, I want to thank Sandy, Lee and Auntie Ann for taking a chance on me and loving me like your own, for welcoming me to Wallasey and making me feel at home.

Dad, you have always been there and for that I'm forever grateful! You are my absolute hero!

I have been somewhat lucky to have been blessed with more than one mum figure in my life.

So, my next dedication goes to Jayne, Bev and Chris you three ladies tried your hardest to love me despite me being impossible to love and I was never just a paycheck to you ladies.

I feel so blessed to have you all in my life even to this day. Each one of you are very dear to me!

Mum and fizzy, you of course get a dedication!
We have one of the most chaotic relationships but without you both I'm totally lost. I love you.

I have made many friends in this life but my longest friend who knows me better than I know myself. Tasha you were and still are my bestest friend, a friendship I will hold close all my life.

I know you'll kill me if you don't get a mention Ann my other oldest friend mwah.

Saving the best till last

My three most treasured people in the whole world my children. Jack, Charlie and Rebecca.   one day you will read mummy's story and feel proud. With everything I do, I do it for you my babies, waiting patiently for the day we are all back together.

I love you all more than words can say,

Steve and Shereen Arbon you have taught me so much and I am the woman, I'm becoming thanks to your patience with me.

My biggest thanks go to God for the Grace he has poured over me. He has surrounded me with a wonderful family that take me as I am.

Like I said before, sorry if I have missed anyone, I love you all xxx

INTRODUCTION

Life! What is the real meaning of life? We work our backsides off all year round to get to the first of January.

To then start the hamster wheel all over again. Making resolutions and goals, convincing ourselves that this year is different...

I have said for a few years now, that I'm going to write a book. Let's face it, I have many stories to share! Living life on that hamster wheel with a job and family drama is a very big step forward from the life I once lived. So, I'm not really complaining.

This time eleven years ago I was hanging on the corner of Shaftsbury Avenue trying to score some crack and heroin. Oh, how my life has changed!

Let me just ask you a question…

Do you ever wonder why? when you see homeless people, standing on the corner blatantly trying to score.

Do you ever think to yourself, that could be your brother or sister there? Or worse, your child?

Truth is, it is someone's brother or sister, son or daughter. That person was someone's little baby once. But somehow, they lost their way in life with nobody there to pull them back on to the right path.

Just recently I have attended a few conferences relating to issues our communities face. Especially homelessness. The truth is homelessness is such a big topic right now, due to its escalation in numbers and it being a prime cause to many deaths.

Finally, people are waking up to the severity of homelessness. People are wanting to help in all areas of the country.

Which is great but first you must truly understand the reasons behind why someone would, and I quote "Choose "to live on the streets.

In this book I want to share with you some of my own stories of being homeless and the lead up to it. In hope to inspire and encourage you to help bring resolutions to the issue once and for all.

There is always a story behind the sad eyes of a beggar, keep on reading if you want to hear mine…

Back when I was at school, they taught us. The best way to start a story is once upon a time. Well I'm not a stick to the rule's kind of person, so, I'm going to do this my way!

My name is Kerri, I would like to say I'm just an ordinary girl, but that would be a big fat lie! My life is far from ordinary and has been one huge rollercoaster of life changing events. Some good, some very traumatic.

The heartbreaking truth I realize is, I'm not the only person, that has had to deal with the struggles that have been thrown my way. I strongly believe that, we should not dwell on things that happen to us in this life. We should use our experience to show others, that there is hope in the darkness.

So many people have told me to write a book, so here goes. Before you dig into my life story though, please be aware, there are things that you may read, that upset you. I'm just being real and honest. Healing comes with vulnerability, someone needs to bare all to give a better understanding of what we are dealing with, in the world of chaos we live in. In order to bring around real resolutions.

I would also like to throw into the mix, that I'm winging the whole writing a book thing! Please forgive me if I come across politically incorrect!

Now, grab yourself a cuppa, maybe even some tissues and get ready to be enlightened and encouraged to make a difference.

CHAPTER ONE – JUST A GIRL

It was the 2nd of May 1984… Obviously I can't remember the day I was born, so I need to give a bit of hearsay for the first part of this chapter. My mum and dad were together when I was born, although unmarried.

They were in an intimate relationship. All I really know about this day is that my name came from a song, that played on my mum's mind. "Hey, Kerri Anne, what's your game now can anybody play?"

It's ironic really because all my life I have played a game of chicken across the tracks. Jumping from gap to gap in life, like a little dare devil so lucky not to fall down the hole. Although I have fallen down that hole many of times. I have always found a way to climb out!

Back to the story though…

Okay, so I was the youngest child of my mothers, she had two other daughters before me. Sadly, my oldest sister died at the very young age of six months. I never got to meet my sister, but there has always been a place in my heart for her.

My other older sister I don't really want to talk about through this book, more for respect for her privacy. I also want to honor my mother the same way. We all have our difficulties in life, who are we to judge another from their mistakes, instead we must learn from them.

My Father was in my life for around ten months, before he and my mother split violently. The split led to me not seeing my father again until later in my life. We will get to that in a bit!

My mother had met a man, shortly after the split with my father. A man she went on to marry. That man became my first stepdad. However, by the time I was eighteen months old. That relationship had also deteriorated due to violence. One thing I will say about my mum is she has the strength of ten men and will give back just as hard as she gets. One of the things I received from her genetics and I'm proud of it!

My mum has her insecurities for her own reasons and who knows she may even write her own book one day! Due to those insecurities she finds it difficult to be alone without a man in her life. Being a single parent was never going to be a label on my mum.

I was around two years and my mum had started a relationship with another man. My mum went on to marry that man and he became my DAD! (You will see my point as you read on) …

I'm going to skip on a couple of years because, my memories are vague, I remember we moved a couple of times, but my real memories began in Bensham Crescent. I can't say specifically how old I was when we moved to Bensham, the school my sister and I went to, was my first actual school so I guess I must have been around five.

My parents seemed happy together we were one big happy family. Dad would talk about adopting us, then came the proposal which my mum accepted. It was perfect.

The Big Day - September 1st 1990…

My sister and I were bridesmaids at the wedding with my auntie. It was a beautiful day. The bridesmaid dress I wore was blue and my hair was in two French plaits. After the ceremony there was a reception for all ages at a local pub. Then later in the evening there was an adult only party.

In the evening when everyone was at the party, my sister and I were being babysat by our great grandmother. She was extremely death and quite elderly and frail.

Along with my great nan there was a cousin through marriage staying over too. A female cousin that was around ten years older than me. I was six at the time of my parents wedding.

The house in Bensham was a three bedroomed property, my sister and I had our own bedrooms. My bedroom was right at the top of the stairs, neighboring the living room.

Whilst lying in bed that evening my thoughts racing ten to the dozen from the day. An excited little six-year-old so happy that we were a proper family.

Mid thought, my bedroom door opened, followed by my cousin peering her head around the corner of my door. "You Ok" She asked as she came in, I don't really know what we talked about, but I just remember that I was quite happy rabbling on to her about the events that had taken place that day. As she climbed into my bed, I felt fine, no reason to be alarmed, right?

This was my cousin it is fine to share a bed. The conversation soon changed as my cousin began to tell me about her pregnancy. She was going to have a baby! This brought me excitement. A natural feeling, I guess.

She went on to say that, when the baby came it would have to drink milk from her breasts. I had no idea what she was talking about I was six, my mother hadn't got to the birds and the bees talk yet.

My cousin asked me to perform oral sex on her. She told me that certain acts would be "Kissing her baby" or testing her breasts for milk. I feel sick just typing this part of my life. For so many years I have felt such shame, but I was only a six-year-old girl!!...

She went on to tell me that it was a secret that she was pregnant, and I couldn't tell anyone, I did as I was told. Even when it became apparent that she wasn't having a baby as time went by, I have always kept her secret. Until now!

I'm sorry to be so graphic it makes me want to hurl reading it too, but to be fair how do you tell that sort of story? This event didn't affect me till years later in my life, and if I'm honest it haunts me to this day, but who knows me sharing this with you, may bring me some healing and freedom, and not to mention in hope that it brings freedom for someone else.

After my mum and dad married, they both worked like dogs to provide for us. Mum had 3 jobs on the go at one point. Although they did their best to provide for us, they were unable to provide us with their time. Something I know they both regret now.

Due to the overbearing work schedule, my nan would look after us. Our day would look like this...

We would wake up, as mum and dad were leaving for work, my nan who lived a few doors away. Would come and get us in our nightdresses to take us to her house.

When we got there, we would get ready for school and have breakfast. Then off we went to school. At three thirty when the school day was over, back we went to nana's house where we would have dinner. Mum and Dad would then come and collect us. Home we went with little time to spare before bed.

My nan had many children including two sets of twins. I don't know exactly how many children my nan bore as she lost some of her offspring through childbirth including one of each set of twins. However, she had five healthy children consisting of three boys and two girls when I was growing up.

The youngest two of her children were teenagers at the time my nana used to look after us. So, they were more like elder siblings than auntie and uncle.

As siblings do, they used to torment me and call me stupid and goad me to tears. They would find amusement in setting the Yorkshire terrier dogs on me by yanking on my cardigan saying "gets, gets"

I remember being dragged down the stairs by the gruesome twosome as my family just laughed. They are the smallest dogs, but boy are they vicious!

I would cry out, which fueled their behavior. In their minds there is no harm, they were just messing, but if I did it to their children. Well, that would be completely different now. I don't hold a grudge, but I will say that I know their behavior was wrong. They were young and didn't really have a clue about the real impact that their constant tormenting was going to have on me.

Around a year after my parent's had married, we moved into an area that was alien to us, it was a house with two great big gardens. Maple Road, one of my favorite homes.

Maple road was a very spacious three-bedroom house. It was my dream home. My sister and I shared a room and the spare room was our playroom. Everything was perfect, we were a real proper family in a real proper family home.

So, I thought! We were too young to see the cracks appearing in my parents' marriage. Around 1992 they split for the first time.

Due to the separation, my mum decided she wanted to move back to her birthplace in East London. So, all packed up, off we went.

Shortly after we arrived in London, we stayed at an old boyfriend of hers flat, behind Bow road police station. He was a nice man, a lot older than my mum but he was nice. It soon became apparent that this was a new boyfriend of my mothers, and that this was now our new family.

I always felt like I was betraying my dad, by playing happy families with someone else but in all honesty, I didn't really understand what was going on. By this time, I was used to different men being around.

We were only there for around six months; I remember celebrating my eighth birthday in that house. Although it was not long after that we moved into a bed and breakfast in Streatham because the relationship had broken down.

Well! Have you ever been in temporary accommodation, provided by the local authority because you were facing homelessness? That is what this bed and breakfast was.

We were homeless! My mum, my sister and me. Just the three of us for the first time ever. The council had placed us into this temporary accommodation. It was disgusting!

My sister would call it bug city! It was one room, basically your average studio room with a little en-suite bathroom attached. Not that anyone would even dare to go in there.

In fear of being bombarded by cockroaches. It really was traumatic, the thought of the bugs crawling all over us while we slept.

The place was overrun by cockroaches. I'm still petrified of the things now.

We only stayed there one night. Then off we went to my grandads' house. My mum's biological father. He was like the BFG so tall and kind. We only stayed there a little while before we moved into a squat around the corner from him.

Over the course of a couple of months my mum became very chaotic in her search to meet the next person we would be calling dad.

So chaotic she would go out on the town and leave us alone with a neighbor looking in on us from time to time.

That's how the music man came along. I'm trying so hard to not mention anyone's names here but even I'm beginning to lose track now.

The music man was called Simon, he was a partner we only met once so it really doesn't matter if I name him. I call him the music man because when we went to his house, there were musical instruments everywhere. We were around 8 and 9 at the time.

The guy was also on top of the pops once too. This was the first relationship to split our family apart. With my mum spending more and more time at Simons we became extremely neglected.

One day my sister had enough of my mum just leaving us overnight to go and see her boyfriend. So, she called my nana, to come and get us.

I remember her sobbing because she had enough. Bearing in mind she was not even a ten-year-old.

What felt like the next day, my nana and uncle were in front of us in our living room getting ready to take us back to Newcastle.

My mum didn't seem too bothered and just let us go. This was the first time my nana applied for custody of my sister and me.

It was around 1993 I was only around nine, we had been living with my nana for a couple of months.

She had applied for a residence order so that she could have complete guardianship for me and my sister.

My mum failing to appear in court automatically gave my nana the rights. It was about six months later that my mum finally came to get us. To which time it was too late.

I remember the day like it was yesterday. I had just got in from school and my nana was waiting. "I've got some good news" she said.

I was excited to hear what she had to tell me. "Your mums coming" she went on to say. I just broke into tears, a flood of emotion just washed over me.

"Why are you crying?" I don't know I replied I'm just happy! In that moment, my nana gave me a hug, she rarely expressed emotion, so I clenched on tighter to keep me topped up until the next time she felt the need to give me a cuddle.

I asked if I could stay up late till mum arrived, but my nana declined. She told me that my mum wouldn't be arriving until it was extremely late. So, no it was completely out of the question.

Although I wasn't allowed to stay up, there was no way that I was getting any sleep that night! I of course was still awake when my mum arrived around midnight.

All those feelings that I expected to feel were nowhere in sight. I felt numb!

My mother was here, sitting right there in front of me. After all this time she was there. Should I hug her I thought to myself, in that thought process, I found myself making way to my mum.

I sat on her knee, it felt weird because I was a big girl now. Almost nine, however a very young nine. It was a very brief moment of reconciliation, before she told me to get off, but it was enough to make me feel something again.

I got sent to bed and was out like a light, feeling content because my mum was home.

My mum was staying at her little sister's house at the bottom of the street, we were living in. My mum was trying her best to convince my nana she was up to parenting my sister and me. She had got a house in

Scotswood which is a little distance from my nanas house in Blaydon. However, mum was determined she wanted us back.

My nana would let us visit at first, then eventually allowed us to go back and live with her.

Before we officially went back to live there, I remember coming home from school and my nana told me she had some news for me. This again? What could it be?

My nana said that my mum was going to take me to meet my dad, I looked at her saying okay, but he only lives down the street. No, she said! Your real dad.

So, basically, she was talking about the man who played a part in my conception. The man who hadn't seen me since I was a babe in arms.

So, it turns out, my biological father lived about three streets away from our new house in Scotswood. When we first arrived at his house, I recall being shy.

Then he pulled out a Sega master system and I was putty in his hands. By the end of the visit he was the best thing since sliced bread. I had two dads now how lucky was I.

As these days played out, I had no idea the impact that it was having on my dad. Not my father but my dad.

The man who had raised me as his own since I was two years old. He is my real dad, my absolute hero! The only man that you will ever hear me call DAD! It is only now that I realize how much it hurt him when I had a brief relationship with my biological father.

I emphasize on the word brief, that is exactly what it was! Brief. It was the year Jurassic Park was on in the cinema, I remember because it was the last place we went for our contact. So, from just before my ninth birthday in May 1993 up until July 1993.

After a quick two-month fix of biological love and then off goes my father. I was very used to change in my life already so; it didn't really faze me that this man I barely knew was gone.

I do remember asking when I was going to see him again though occasionally as time went by. We lived in three houses in Scotswood, two that were more or less next door to each other. The third house was about five streets away. That house…

I recall as the house of horrors.

CHAPTER TWO – HOUSE OF HORRORS

We moved to the third house I think in the late summer of 1993. It was around the same time the contact ended with my biological father. My mum had done a 360-degree spin and was now more chaotic than her last breakdown in London.

Like before, mum would go out once a week on the town, Thursdays to be exact, leaving us to fend for ourselves, with a neighbor looking in. We were older now; I was nine and my sister would be eleven at the end of the summer.

Not quite old enough to be left alone till the early hours of the morning, but like I said my mum has always had her own demons to face.

I also want to add that my mum was diagnosed with bipolar disorder when I was around seventeen! So, I ask you to please consider this fact as you continue to read on.

Back to the story though!

Okay, picture the scene… A nine-year-old with no boundaries, left home alone with no parental guidance. If you picture the kid from problem child and put him in the movie home alone, you may see where I'm going with this.

So, every Thursday mum would get ready to go out on the town. She would have a bath; blow dry her hair then fix up her makeup and off she went as regular as clockwork.

When she went out, she would ask the neighbor in the downstairs flat to look in on us. At first it was all safe and sound, we would play out till it got dark then come in and later go to sleep in mums bed awaiting her return. Over a space of about two months this occurred.

Now, where we lived was one of the roughest parts of Newcastle. So, it's safe to say I was easily influenced by poor peer choices.

Let's face it, all I had witnessed in my life up until now, Bad Ass was becoming first nature.

I used to get up to all sorts from smoking the joints my mum left in the ashtray, to joining the bigger kids in the street as they got up to mischief.

After about three weeks, one night my mum came home drunk, stripped and got straight into bed.

Then in the early hours of the morning she was awoken by a man in the bedroom crouched at her bed, trying to cut the rings off her fingers, she had at least one on each finger. When she woke up, she automatically jumped up and chased the man out of the house and halfway down the street, completely oblivious to the fact she was naked.

Now, I would personally like to think that would have been the awakening needed for her behavior to change. Unfortunately, that was not the case.

Due to this incident, my dad had let us look after his rottweiler Bruno. He was as soft as muck but hopefully, due to his breeds reputation his bark would be enough of a scare tactic to keep burglars at bay.

The following week mum had decided to go out again, and left us on our own with the neighbor looking in.

It was all good because, we had Bruno now too, it was all going to be completely safe and above board. As usual mum came into us sleeping in her bed, where she would join us.

I'm not quite sure what happened this night but somehow, someone managed to break in. Only this time they stole my dad's baby! Yup, they took the dog.

Bruno was a first-year wedding anniversary present from my mum. My dad adored him! He was a full pedigree rottweiler, and the perfect example of man's best friend. As you can imagine my dad was absolutely devastated.

After a short time, it could have been days or maybe even over a week later, the lady who lived downstairs that would watch in on us, informed my mum she knew where Bruno was.

I don't know the whole in's and out, but I remember the woman's cousin Lee was an absolute hero because he somehow managed to retrieve our Bruno.

To prevent anything like this happening again my dad took Bruno home that night, so we were back to just being three vulnerable females under one roof.

Around two weeks later after a brief retreat, mum had decided she was going out. It was Thursday and it had been a couple of weeks.

This time was different though! This time she asked the lady downstairs to babysit us properly. It's strange because I remember so clearly of this night.

We went to the lady's relatives house for some reason. To which Lee came into the house, the man who got our dog back. Apparently, he lived there. I remember him making a big spectacle about getting in the bath, like he wanted us to know that's where he was.

It seemed like a very long time that he was in there, but when he returned, he looked exactly as he did when he left. His hair was dry and clothes the same. Even at nine years old I was extremely observant, I have no idea why, but It does come in useful though.

Not long after Lee returned from the bathroom, it was time for us to go home. It was Lee and his girlfriend that took us back. Upon walking up the stairs we knew something wasn't quite right. Then, we reached the living room to find that we had been completely burgled.

With no mobile phones in those days, just the good old-fashioned land line there was no way of contacting my mum, so we just had to wait till she came home.

To be honest most of the night from that point on is a bit of a blur, maybe because that was a memory, I have desperately tried so hard to forget. Not long after that night though we finally moved! Back to Blaydon into the same street as my Nana.

Rebelling from traumatic events, my mother and I began to clash big time! I resented her so much. I had zero respect towards her, and she had no authority over me.

I just wanted the woman to love me, but she didn't know how. But she knew how to love my sister which irritated me even more.

Christmas came and went then a New Year came, that was the year of 1994.

CHAPTER THREE – WHO CARES?

It was early 1994, my auntie and her sister in law decided to take a trip to London to visit my cousin Shell. On that visit, my auntie met a man and started a long-distance relationship. Then, the man and his friend came to visit my auntie at her home in Newcastle.

After a short time, my auntie moved to Erith in Kent to live with the man. Not long after my mum took us for a three-week holiday during summer break. In which time she started a relationship with my aunties, boyfriends, friend, who came to Newcastle that time. I know it all sounds confusing! Right? Wait till you read on later it gets a whole lot more confusing!

During our three-week holiday, mum had decided that she too wanted to move to Kent, and that thought very quickly materialized into a move into her new boyfriends house.

Wow did this anger me! I hated the fact my mum had once again just picked us up and carried us three hundred miles and taken us away from my dad. All for another man! How dare she!

I started a primary school at the end of our street in the September 1994, I hated that too! I was bullied for the whole year I was there because I was different. Having a very strong Geordie accent, nobody could understand me, which led to even more ridicule.

Trying so desperate to fit in, I would do things that were wrong, like smoke, steal and cause trouble. All to make me look good in front of the cool kids, trying my best to claim acceptance.

Along with the mischief came constant battles with

my mum and then one day she just flipped.

It was sometime in 1995, I was approaching eleven years old, somehow volatile yet innocent. I was angered by mum so easily. One day she had caught me with one of her lighters and just lost control.

Then she walked into the kitchen, after giving me a hiding, she slit her wrists, then called social services and told them to come and get me. My mum was desperate, saying if you don't come and get her, I'll either hurt her or myself.

After a short period of time we had to attend a meeting at the Howbury Centre. As we waited in the lobby, there was a lady with a little mixed raced boy, he was around two with a head full of curly hair. I have always loved babies and toddlers, a natural instinct within me would arise to interact with the little people. I played with the little boy as we waited, my mum looked so lovingly at the little boy too. It is weird because I know my mum loves me in her weird way, but she never looked at me the same way.

Something else I have always resented is the fact my mum always shows love to other people's kids but never the same for me. Like I said though, I know she loves me in her own way, so I'm kind of over that now.

Back to the story! As we waited, and I played with the little boy. I remember thinking how it would be nice to live with this lady and her little boy. When the social worker came in, she said shall we go through, to my joy! Jayne and Danny came in too.

I was over the moon! I felt bad on my mum, but it was as if she didn't want me, so it was okay. At least I was going to live with someone that was nice, and that I already liked!

Jaynes house was different, it was filled with peace and love, not like the hippy kind, but the kind of warm peaceful family love. It felt so natural.

It very quickly became apparent that Jayne and Glen her husband were Christian's. Every Sunday they would attend a little Pentecostal Church in Woolwich, South East London. I absolutely loved it.

Everyone would dance up and down the aisles, singing Hallelujah, Praise the Lord. Is was fire! I had never seen such joy in all of my life.

Each week we went, and I loved it more and more. So, I asked my mum if I could be baptized, she declined stating if God was real, why did Rebecca die? At that age I had no answer to such a question, so I never asked again.

I lived there well over a year; I was actually sad to leave when I returned to my mum's care.

However, I was only home with my mum a matter of weeks before I was back in care at Jaynes house. Only this time was different, she had two other girls with special needs, that required her undivided attention.

I became very insecure and felt as though I was unwanted, the second time round. That was the beginning of my runaway days.

I left Jaynes care and that was the start of many placements to come. Placement's where there was no love, just selfish motive. The more I moved around, the more unstable I became.

Running away at every opportunity I became what is known as a prolific absconder. I hated being in care, I hated the fact that I was so easily discarded yet, my older sibling was held so close like a porcelain doll.

I wanted to be at home with my real mum, instead of with the pretend wannabes the social worker kept placing me with. To be honest when I look back, I think what a little minx I was, always thought I knew what was best. Bold and stubborn were a trait that I had not yet mastered.

CHAPTER FOUR - RUNAWAY

The first time I ever slept rough, I was around thirteen years old. I'd run away from a foster placement to go up west. I loved going to the west end in hunt for famous people. My favorite haunt was sound republic, opposite Leicester Square.

Back in the nineties they used to host MTV select there, you were guaranteed to see someone famous. I actually believed that I would one day become famous if I hung out there long enough.

I often stayed up west till the last train, but something was different this day. I can't remember exactly why, but I knew I was not going home.

I had made lots of friends on the street mainly through the soup vans that used to attend the Strand every night. We were like a family all looking out for each other. I did get a slap once for being too young. I was told to go home, that I didn't belong there. The truth is, that was the only place in my mind, I did belong.

As the years went by, I became quite popular with the police. They would come and remove me from my begging spot outside the NatWest bank on the strand, to take me home to my current foster carers.

I used to find it quite amusing, they would drop me off home and by the time they got back to their patrol on the Strand, I would be sitting in the very same spot, begging for my McDonalds. Yes, I know! Good way to spend taxes! I'm only joking.

I'm not denying I was an absolute little bitch. I even got Bitch No.1 tattooed on my arm at aged fifteen, thinking it was clever. Oooh, if I knew then what I know now!!

I feel like this is a good point to highlight the fact that I was a kid with no morals or awareness of boundaries, nor did I have any ability to consider the ethics behind my behavior.

I had no love shown to me as a child, I was just a big inconvenience to all. Cast aside like an old boot, as my grandad used to say.

I continued to run away on a regular basis, to which point social services had run out of placements to house me in.

Which was when I moved to Eastbourne in East Sussex, the one place that I somehow managed to settle in. Miles away from the west end, and miles away from my family, a clean break from everything.

The thing is, I was not impressed with this move! There was no way I was moving all this way. My poor social worker Eileen had to listen to me cursing all the way from Slade Green in Kent to this new foster placement on the seafront of Eastbourne, which was approximately an hour's drive away.

When we pulled up outside this huge four-story house on the seafront, I dug my heels into my seat and refused to get out of the car. At this time in my life I was almost fourteen and full of bad attitude.

I had become the master at wrapping social workers around my little finger. For sure this was going to work, Eileen would get fed up with waiting and eventually, she will take me home, she can't physically move me.

I so had this! The next thing I knew there was a lady outside the car, she knocked on the window and asked if I wanted a fag?

I just remember being so taken back by this lady who didn't know me from adman, yet she knew exactly how to calm me right there and then.

The truth is behind the bad attitude I was just a girl, craving for someone to get me. Someone to understand me. Heck let's be honest I just needed to feel like someone loved me and not the hefty paycheck.

The lady gave me a cigarette and reassured me that everything was going to be ok. We both stood up from the curb, I took a deep breath and went into my new home with my new foster mum Bev…

"So, there I was in my lounge with a couple of social workers. "I'm sorry, said Kerry's social worker. She's refusing to come in. I looked out the window, my heart tweaked. That poor girl, it's not surprising, sat in the car across the road I could see the figure of a teenaged girl in the car head down. We waited. She never came in. I grabbed a packet of cigarettes left the house crossed the road, knocked on the car window. 'Would you like a cigarette, I'm Bev" You looked at me, I felt you were weighing me up for a second. You got out the car and we sat on the edge of the pavement and short conversation that I can't quite remember. You decided to come in. Moving on several months, and after a few hiccups I won't mention unless you want me to privately. You definitely changed it was a slow change but a change, nevertheless. You appeared a little more in control. Little easier to reason with. Less angry with yourself. We will always have a soft spot for Kerri. X "

Beverly Arkle

I shocked many people whilst living at this placement I was part of the family unit for around eighteen months before things started to turn sour. I became extremely close to Bev, so close she was like a proper mum to me.

The only thing was, I wasn't her only foster child. When new kids came, I felt threatened and intimidated not to mention the fact I was a hormonal teenager.

I never got on with other kids in care, the worst was when I lived in the kid's homes, I was always fighting and getting kicked out for going too far.

My natural response was hurt before you get hurt. So, when new kids came to Bev's that same instinct would surface.

Only I didn't hurt the kids, I hurt the care giver instead. I still have regrets of my behavior towards the end of my placement at Bev's house.

I was fifteen when I officially left Bev's care, I remember us both being devastated by my destruction. Destruction became my middle name from then on…

Eileen had found me a placement in Abbey Wood, they were brand new foster carers and couldn't wait to have me. If only they knew then what they knew now…

I was a nightmare for them. Chris was the nicest lady, with such a heart of gold. Ray was a bit firmer, he scared me a little in a dad kind of way.

Nevertheless, they were so kind and caring, and me being me I took advantage.

A few days before my 16th birthday I decided to run away and join the fun fair. I had met a guy and fallen in love, besotted was an understatement.

I was prepared to give up everything and travel the fair with him. The thing was, he wasn't that into me.

We travelled from west end to Hereford which is where he literally binned me off. Although I'm the sort of person to wear my heart on my sleeve, my tolerance to emotional pain is phenomenal. I guess it's all those years of feeling unloved by the people who should love you.

So, there I was in Hereford feeling pretty sorry for myself, whilst poor Chris was at home worried sick about me.

Having been missing for days on end. I had to go home, with a huge slice of humble pie. I remember I had been wearing a white outfit for days, it stunk and was filthy with dirt.

I remember the looks of horror on the train from Manchester Piccadilly all the way to Charing Cross as I sat in squalor with my head down in shame. Upon arrival at London Charing Cross I made way to Charing cross police station.

I knew that if I represented myself as a runaway, they would call the emergency social worker, who would then call my carers.

I remember the moment when Chris saw me again, she was just so relieved to see me safe and well. I'd never seen that look of relief in someone's eye before, this woman actually cared about me!

Unfortunately, I was beyond control at this point, and my time a Chris and Ray's house was short lived. Chris in particular has always had a place in my heart though, even to this day she is a part of my life, encouraging me into greatness.

My childhood and upbringing were key in what you are about to read in the next chapter. Behavior is learnt and unfortunately the only behavior I ever learnt growing up, was how to be unstable.

With no idea on how to stay in one place for a long period, my idea of settlement was being on my toes. By the time I was seventeen all services had been immaturely discharged.

Despite being under a full care plan until I was twenty-one, I was released from care with no place to go. I showed no signs of stability, therefore the local authority had no more they could offer me.

When you get discharged from care, you move into supported accommodation. It is either a shared house with other care leavers or someone who owns a house, lets you live there under agreement with the leaving care team.

I had a different social worker; her name was Janis and boy did she put up with some crap from me. She housed me in a few supported lodgings, but somehow, I would mess it up.

I had no rules, no boundaries and no curfew but I did have a key and an uncontrollable urge to do whatever I wanted.

I had complete freedom; nobody was ever going to tell me what to do ever again! The only thing is, it's not as good as it sounds.

I would go up west for nights on end, begging to make some money, to buy my shopping. Or I would join the fair when it was in season.

Then leave at the end of the season. To end up on the doorstep of the leaving care team at the howbury center in Slade Green, Kent.

I would sit in the lobby for hours on end, demanding to see Janis my social worker or Jacquie the manager. I needed a placement and I wasn't going anywhere until I got it.

Fortunately for me I was under a full care plan, and the local authority were my legal guardians and had no choice but to accommodate me until I was twenty-one.

Which by the way they neglected to maintain in a different area of the country!

So, here I was seventeen, full of hurt, resentment and anger against the world for not loving me. I became more settled in, sleeping under Charing Cross train station.

With a street family who got me. This is where I belonged. This was my destiny; I was living the real life of the artful dodger.

When I was sleeping under the train station, I began a relationship with a guy called trigger.

I had experienced crack for the first time, and we became partners in selling the Big Issue to raise money for the drug.

We were never intimate more like best friends, I was what you call frigid and never wanted to go all the way. In fact, I was so frigid I never even snogged him.

After a couple of weeks of waking up having a pipe, running around on the hamster wheel that came with the addiction.

Beg, score, be high for twenty minutes and then go and do it all again. It quickly became unbearable. So, hating myself and the life I was living, it was time for me to call on my family.

Well, my older sister to be precise. I called my sister one day and asked if I could go and stay with her for a couple of days, which to my surprise she agreed to. However, soon the novelty wore off and she became tired of me just being around doing nothing.

CHAPTER FIVE – HOME

Engaging with the social services in Gateshead, my place of birth. It was not long before I had bagged myself a tidy little two bedroom flat, in the street behind my sister's house.

It was going to be amazing! It was going to be different! I was going to get my act together and grow up!

Guess how long that lasted!!

Not long at all! I was associating with all the wrong people, people who understood me.

Alcoholics, glue sniffers all those who come from a life they want to hide from. I started hanging around with this one guy in particular. He was addicted to solvents and had nowhere to live. So, I offered refuge at my flat as it was too big for just me.

The man became scary, I was too afraid to tell him to leave me alone. The icing on the cake though, was when I visited Kent for a Christmas party at the howbury center.

I loved the Christmas parties, there was always a karaoke, so I'd be on that all night long.

Upon returning to Gateshead, I got the fright of my life! I got home to find the man I had so eagerly tried to evict.

I had previously retrieved my spare key from him, so I was confused at how he had got in. Well, he broke in. climbed up the drainpipe and in the kitchen window. He knew I was away so squatted in my house. He then refused to leave, which involved me informing the police.

No longer feeling safe I decided to up and leave again, returning to Kent. I was then housed in a supported accommodation in Gravesend by the homeless department in Bexley Heath.

There was no support about it though. It was basically a three-bedroom house share with a shared lounge and kitchen. No support network, or service.

Well, actually, to be fair! I have a feeling the support was there, but nobody there to encourage and love me. That was until Liz and Pat moved in.

The couple took me under there wing, they loved me and cared for me like I was one of their own. I used to go on errands with them and eat with them, watch tv in the evenings with them. I was growing to love them. Do you remember me saying previously, that I was naïve? Well, get on this!

Everyday we would go shopping with Neil and Mel, a couple that were always around. Mel hated me for some reason and I never knew why.

She always smoked this stuff on tin foil, one day I asked her what it was. To which she replied it was just cannabis resin.

The issue was never raised again. After "Shopping" we would have to stop off at the chemist every day, to pick up Pat's prescription. Another thing I never questioned…

To top it off! One day I walked into the room and Liz was injecting something into Pat's arm, this I did question, and Liz replied that it was medicine and that he needed it, so he didn't get sick. I STILL didn't cotton on.

Three of them were shoplifting, heroin addicts taking me on missions and to score at seventeen years old. The new family I trusted were liars!

That wasn't what made me leave though! Liz was a lot older than Pat and she was severely disabled.

Not to mention quite minted being on the high rate of DLA. Pat was a prolific drug user, criminal and in honesty he was just disgusting.

One day, we went out for a drive somewhere, just Pat and me. He offered to give me a driving lesson, and told me to climb between his legs, to reach the pedals.

Innocently I did so! He then began to try and kiss my neck, to which I almost drove into the tree. I asked him what he was doing? He responded telling me he loved me! I was mortified and told him to take me home.

Days later after a whole lot of awkwardness, I felt like I had betrayed Liz. She was the only decent one out of them. It was fairground season, and I had heard that there was a site not so far away.

So off I went with my troubles in my old kit bag and joined the fair again, only this time I travelled for a longer period of time.

Fairground life is really NOT!! As FUN as you would imagine. Yes, it's fun for those enjoying the rides, not fun for us building them up and pulling them down every few days.

It was a hard graft with no sex discrimination act in sight. I was treated like one of the men. Well, unless my boss Henry was hollering "Get your ***'s out". When it came to work, I was one of the men.

We were doing a ground in Danson Park in Bexley heath, it was on the last day, when we were pulling down.

It was my first real experience of love at first sight. I was pulling down the juvenile and helping on the dodgems. There was a guy called Marc who worked on the waltzer, it was a brief encounter but I undoubtably felt a spark.

Apparently, so did he.

To my delight, the next day, as we were building up on the new sight, I looked up to see Marc across the field. It turned out that he was going to be doing the next couple of grounds with us in Essex. In that time, we spent every spare moment together.

We fell in love like a soppy romantic chick flick. At the end of the season we would spend all of our time in the trailer yard or down the local pub. I was totally head over heels in love with him.

He was a good one. When the new season began Marc and I were going to be separated for a couple of weeks, but we spoke everyday on the phone.

I longed to see him again, and I counted the days till it happened. If only he could have been so patient!

I was doing a ground in Blackheath, and Marc was in Tottenham, Henry was really getting on my nerves with his derogatory comments.

One day I told him to f-off and he sacked me. So, off I went to Tottenham to get a job with one of Marcs bosses. Whilst I was there, I discovered that Marc was actually cheating on me.

So, hurting him more than him hurting me I decided to physically lay into him. I was like a lunatic punching him as he found the whole thing amusing.

I left the next day and never saw him again. Off up west feeling betrayed and alone, unsure of what I was going to do next. Somehow, I ended up in the lobby off the leaving care team back in Gateshead, pleading for help.

Gateshead Social Services were less patient with me, than the howbury center. They sent me straight to the Civic Center to apply as homeless. Having a strong connection in the area and being eighteen, the housing took on my case.

After some time in a hostel in Low Fell and an attempted suicide I was placed into the local psychiatric unit in the Queen Elizabeth Hospital.

CHAPTER SIX – MENTALLY CHALLENGED

My very first suicide attempt was when I was thirteen. I had been sent to an Indian family, which mortified me and there was nothing I could do. Let's just clarify I'm not a racist, something just didn't sit right with me living in this Muslim home.

Due to this attempt on my life, I was labelled mentally challenged. So, when I took a load of pills in the hostel, I was automatically sectioned. I was young, and very immature and the support I got in hospital made me feel safe.

Not to mention that the hospital was right next to my dad's house, so I would get constant visits from him. My dad is the only one who ever really cared. Unfortunately, because he was only my stepdad, my mum restricted the amount of help she would allow him to offer me.

Not to mention the fact that he put up with so much hurt from me.

Whilst sectioned I went through some pretty intense therapy sessions, where I began to reveal my secrets, but then I would close up at the first sign of hurt. Nobody could ever understand how my heart was shattered into pieces.

How the secret of what that horrible woman did to me as a little girl. The abandonment of the people that were supposed to love me no matter what.

The nurses would often find me sleeping under my bed, not understanding why, they just labeled me depressed and anxious. With no idea what I see in my dreams, the things that hurt me and scared me. I wasn't just depressed! I was traumatized.

After spending six or more weeks in the tranwell unit and some sofa surfing at my dad's house, I finally got a new one bedroom flat in Felling, Gateshead. It was a ten-minute walk from my dad's house, it was perfect.

A short time of mixing with the wrong people, I found myself pregnant as a result of a one-night stand.

Wow! Finally! I was going to have unconditional love. Sadly, it was short lived due to a miscarriage at twelve weeks.

So, you know that tolerance to pain I mentioned earlier? This devastated me! I wanted to be a mum so bad.

Not long after my mum moved up to the North East because she had split up with her partner. My dad allowed her to stay in the spare room.

She took advantage and ended up in the hospital herself. I can't quite remember all the details, but somehow, she was sectioned.

Whilst in hospital I would visit her every day, and we actually grew quite close. We have periods where we can be so loving towards each other, then bam world war three kicks off.

When my mum was discharged from hospital, she was given a two-bedroom flat in the Centre of Gateshead. Despite a few hurdles we grew closer and became more and more excited as Christmas got closer.

Although we were both skint and only had a meal and a spliff between us, it was a very nice Christmas. Over the Christmas, mum had received contact from an old friend in Lewisham.

He was staying at a pub that needed staff for new years eve and my mum being a qualified bar manager she jumped at the chance.

When my mum informed me of her plan to go to London for a couple of days, I jumped straight on the band wagon.

London, for New Years, I'll have some of that! I had it all mapped out in my head, I would get there and spend the night begging on the strand in my old pitch.

Within a few days, once the social book was cashed, and the tickets were paid for. There was me and mum on the late coach to London. Both of us excited in our own way mum was going to work in a pub, and I was going up west to see my old friends #Reunion.

I arrived up west and headed straight for the Strand, it was late in the afternoon by now, I'd spent most of the day with my mum at the pub she was going to be working in.

when I arrived on the Strand, I was delighted to see my street brother Ben, a few years younger than me, I used to call him my little brother.

He was sat with two other men, Andy and Paul brothers from Peterlee near Durham. Speaking broad Geordie, I sparked the interest of the elder brother Paul, who was thirty-six years old.

Andy was much younger than his brother, he was around twenty.

After some long conversations and time with Paul, I became quite fond of him and the next thing I knew we were kissing. Not something that I usually do, kiss a stranger! Something was in his eyes though. Something that made me want to love him, care for him, and save him.

Sitting reflecting on the coach as we pulled out of London Victoria Station, returning home from our very brief trip.

I realized that I had to come back soon. I could come back to London, pick him up and take him back to my flat in felling. That is exactly what happened.

Not even forty-eight hours later I'm back behind the theatre at St. Martin's in the field, collecting the man I thought I was destined to save. To my horror as I approached the place he slept.

I found him coming out of a red phone box with a needle hanging from his groin.

This didn't faze me in the slightest, I still thought I could save him. As weeks past in Newcastle, Paul became sly and would use behind my back at every opportunity.

Finding out I was pregnant, didn't stop him either. Six weeks into the pregnancy, he decided enough was enough. He cashed his giro, left me standing on the street corner as he dashed for the coach station.

I was devastated! how dare he! I couldn't believe this no-good waste of space had left me and his unborn son, to go and be with his first love heroin.

After around half an hour waiting on the corner of felling high street, I decided to take a trip to the social services. I hadn't yet informed them of my current predicament, so found this a great opportunity to do so.

I told my social worker all about the pregnancy, and how Paul had just abandoned me. I went on to tell her that my mum was still in London and that I wanted to go and see her and tell her I was pregnant.

A travel warrant was issued, and I jumped on the 3pm train getting me into Charing Cross around 7pm. When I arrived, I couldn't wait to tell everybody of this horrible turn of events.

Andy especially was mortified at his big brothers' behavior. I was curious as to why Paul hadn't come back to Charing cross, surely, he would have no choice?

The next morning, I was awoken by a whisper "Andy, psst Andy" I jumped up to find Paul standing there looking back in sheer horror. The look of how is she here? Its actually quite comical to be fair, looking back on the moment. After a week or so chasing the drugs in London, Paul chose to return to Newcastle with me to make a proper go of it. Just the three of us.

CHAPTER SEVEN – ADDICTED

After all of the exposure to heroin that I have witnessed, it finally got me. I was nineteen and pregnant.

Paul my partner was a serious heroin addict and loved to get me out begging to make money for his addiction.

Growing more and more curious, I one day asked him what was the deal with this drug? He said, it takes your cares away and its just like smoking a joint.

He offered me some on the foil, I had nothing to lose. I had already been informed that my child was being removed from my care by the local authority due to my chaotic history.

Meaning that I was too unstable and unsettled to be able to parent my unborn child.

This fact destroyed me, yes, I was unsettled, but all I ever wanted to be was a mum, to feel unconditional love. Instead that was being ripped away from me by the local authority because they apparently knew best.

All I ever needed was someone to believe in me.

I became addicted very quickly and our habit grew larger as the two of us were now using at least three bags each a day.

We had moved into a temporary bed and breakfast due to becoming homeless when my mum kicked us out.

Paul had turned her house into a smack den, so she told us to leave and she moved back from London to save her flat.

It was a matter of days before we were asked to leave the little bed and breakfast, and we were forced to sleep on the streets.

With all options and resources being exhausted, there was little we could do. I didn't want to ask social services for help, they were taking my baby, I didn't trust them as far as I could throw them.

Here we were! addicted, pregnant and homeless.

As the habit grew bigger, along with my bump, we became more noticeable in the shops we were stealing from to buy our gear.

We were becoming sloppy and cocky which inevitably led to our arrest. It was my first adult offence, so I got away with a caution, Paul on the other hand was a known criminal so was immediately remanded into custody. I was devastated, with no clue as to what I was going to do.

Here I was, all alone, no place to call home. I made my way to a mutual friend's house; I knew she could help me get out of trouble. She had given me some gear and some sound advice.

She then helped me get somewhere to stay in an area that was alien to me. I only stayed there two days as I slowly detoxed on some subitex the girl had given me.

Feeling devastated at the consequences of my actions, it was time to eat an enormous amount of humble pie. I made way to Gateshead leaving care team to beg them for help, no longer caring about trust issues. The time had come for me to get my act together, my unborn son was owed much more than what he was already receiving.

When I explained all to Alison, my social worker at the time, she was deeply concerned for the wellbeing of my child. She made some calls and I was admitted into the Queen Elizabeth Hospital onto the pre-natal ward. I was to remain there until the baby was born.

During my stay at the Queen Elizabeth, I was determined to break free from heroin, and my recovery was on track. It was as if I was living in some fantasy bubble. Paul would be released any day; he would be clean from his forced prison detox. I had been clean two weeks from my hospital detox, it was a winner, winner chicken dinner scenario.

If only the same scenario could have existed in Paul's head! As soon as he got out, the first thing he said to me, was shall we go and score?! That was the first relapse. Temptation waved under my nose for the first time in sixteen day's and I caved! What an idiot!

I was so blinded by love, it was a pretend love, but it was love all the same. All my hard work was undone by that one fix! Paul didn't care that we had just managed a sixteen-day detox, he had no intention of getting clean. I was still determined though!

It was around six weeks between Paul's release and the birth of our son. Jack Paul was born on Tuesday 5th October weighing 6lb 9oz. Becoming a mother was the most magical moment of my life, looking down at my perfect little boy. The hatred I had felt towards the world for so many years, replaced with unconditional love. The joy was short lived through; I was only

going to be this beautiful baby boys' mother for a
matter of days.

It was around twenty-four hours before the headache really kicked in. I had been moved to a side room due to my special circumstances shall we say.

I'd been getting mild headaches which the doctors were reluctant to treat, due to my previous opiate addiction. Then! It just hit me like a wrecking ball.

Due to the epidural piercing a hole in my spine, spinal fluids were leaking to my brain. This is what was causing the headaches, and extreme discomfort.

The only way to treat this rare issue, was to do a spinal procedure to inject blood into the hole. The procedure didn't work the first time, so it had to be done twice. The headaches were so unbearable and the pain in my spine was of the same, I was crippled!

Despite being in all this pain I was still not giving in; I wasn't going to take the one pure painkiller that Paul was willing to prescribe.

It didn't stop him using though! He would have a hit in the toilet when he visited us in the hospital. Jack had been moved to special care to be monitored for methadone withdrawal and because I was in no fit state to care for him.

One day, the nurses were in my room doing my observations. They found a needle with some liquid in it and asked me what it was.

Completely stunned as I had no idea it was there, I replied with "what does it look like" in my defense I was also high on codeine, that the doctor had finally prescribed me.

Not able to completely comprehend the situation, upon further questioning I took the blame for the needle. One of those moments where I look back in my life and literally just want to punch myself in the face. To my complete shock I was arrested, and Paul was nowhere to be seen.

Still in agony from my epidural crisis, I was escorted off of the hospital premises by the police. Arrested for possession, the police took me to the custody sweate at Gateshead police station. I must have zonked out on the meds, as soon as my head hit the rubber pillow!

I was awoken by a guard, he called me out to be charged with the crime. Still hobbling, with my head down in pain I slowly walked to the desk sergeant. I was being released with a caution, it was a minor charge, with no need for further action.

Released in the cold, on a night in early October with no place to go. I was in the same pajamas that I had been wearing for four or five days. They were soiled with blood and I hadn't showered!

My dignity was lost and so was my parental responsibility. Due to this turn of event's there was no way social services were going to allow me to have any rights to Jack.

Totally devastated, I made way to a place behind the high street where Paul and I used to sleep. To my amazement, when I arrived there, I found Paul bedding down.

I was completely overwhelmed! Distraught by the consequences of my actions, I just needed a cuddle. I didn't care that he had hidden and watched throughout the whole ordeal of me being arrested.

Discharged from hospital due to a possession charge, I was not allowed to visit Jack without security present. Something that was meant to be magical, was turned into something so shameful.

The social services had won a court order, and Jack was discharged into their care. The next two months were unbearable, the constant battles, my grandfather dying.

I became too weak to fight anymore and my addiction was back and stronger than ever.

CHAPTER EIGHT – STREETLIFE

It was Christmas time 2004, Jack's first Christmas. I knew it was going to be tough, celebrating without him so I just took enough gear to block it all out. Or I cried myself to sleep, because I couldn't nurse my crying baby, because someone else was.

I had never felt such pain, and it wasn't going away.

Paul and I decided we needed to get away, so we chose to return to London. Despite not having anywhere to go, we didn't care it had to be better than where we were. Jack was being looked after, and we weren't going away for long.

So, we thought! We actually never came back!

We landed in London Victoria around 6am in the morning, we got the late coach and slept the whole way from Newcastle to London. As soon as we arrived, we headed straight to score, we had no worries just freedom.

A pocket full of cash and a habit to feed, we wandered around Tottenham court road to find an early morning shotter.

When we finally scored, we scored some crack too. Paul put the heroin and crack together to create a snowball.

The max effect! The buzz was so euphoric, I was hooked on the first hit. Unaware at the time how addictive this new combination was, it wasn't long before I was completely addicted, and we were taking hundreds of pounds worth a day.

Early 2005 we were officially, street homeless in Piccadilly. Taking £60 worth of snowballs every two hours. The pain was no longer existent, and the thoughts of losing my son were a memory now stored away.

All that motivated me was my next fix, begging was profitable for me because of my fresh face and sad eyes. As the habit grew larger though, so did our confidence to shoplift again.

As time went on, I began to resent Paul, he was like a leech. He'd be up my bum if I was providing the money, soon as I wasn't making any I was beaten and spat on.

Crack and heroin are like an evil spirit, possessing anyone who consumes it.

Now, would be a good time to point out although I may be s big softy at heart, I took no rubbish from anyone! So, if I got hit, he was getting hit back.

It was around a year after we landed in London, that I finally left Paul. My love for drugs had removed any glimmer of thought for anything or anyone else. He was sent to prison on a warrant, which was my get out of jail free card.

We had moved into a St. Mungos hostel on Endel Street, just before his arrest. The hostel had an inhouse substance misuse clinic, and a support team in every area of need.

I personally took advantage and got myself on a methadone script. Crack was my drug of choice now, heroin just held me back with the sickness that came along with it.

Now Paul was out of my way, there was no stopping me! I would shoplift all day, selling my stuff to the brasses, in the flats on Wardour Street.

From perfumes to Radley handbags I was on a mission. I would graft on Oxford Street, sell on Wardour Street and score on Dean Street all within an hour. I was on fire, and cocky with it!

The trouble is when you become invisible in your mind, from the crack. The more noticeable you are to the world around you.

After a short time, I was back on the streets, all alone on Piccadilly. The constant crack use had got me kicked out of the hostel, more for my attitude whilst being under the

Influence rather than being on the substance itself. Nobody liked me, I was always upsetting people. Apart from one person, the next love of my life, Slasher.

Slasher and I met, whilst I was still with Paul. There was an instant spark, but I always stayed faithful to Paul, even though I always knew that slasher would treat me better.

Slasher would always tell me how beautiful I was and how if I was his girl, he would treat me like a princess. I can't deny, although I was faithful, I longed for a day that I could be slashers girl.

When I finally left Paul, I wasn't interested in being tied down with someone else.

I did spend time with slasher, and we did grow closer, but we were too far into the friend's zone, it felt weird to go beyond that now. Until this happened…

It was Christmas week 2006, I was begging in my usual spot at the Alliance and Leicester on Piccadilly.

The money people gave at Christmas time was unreal. It would take me about twenty minutes to make twenty pounds, it was like a pound a minute. Unfortunately, along with the rise in generosity, came a rise in police patrol.

I was just casually sitting, not even being volatile, when a car pulls up. Two plain clothes officers jump out of the car, all dramatic and nick me on the spot. Before I could blink, I was standing in custody, being read my rights.

Pulling out the mental health card, I pleaded suicidal, which led to me being released without charge into the care of the Westminster Psychiatric Unit on a 48hr section for an assessment.

Well, psychotic was an understatement! I wanted out, from the minute I arrived. The ward was run by very large, hospital staff nurses.

Most were African and didn't take no crap from anyone. I really was a weed compared to them! It didn't stop me coming up against them though. A mixture of men and women but equal in strength all the same.

I made way for the door on many occasions within the next 48hrs, without success. It was the most excruciating time of my life! I was forced to have a shower by the women, when I say forced, I mean forced! Pinned down, fully clothed scrubbed with shampoo and very lukewarm water.

I kicked off like a wild animal which resulted in me getting a large shot of chlorpromazine in my backside that instantly knocked me out. When it finally wore off, I was free to go…

Still in a haze from the chlorpromazine and looking like a scarecrow I made my way up west. The hospital was only in Victoria, so I just jumped on the 453 bus to Piccadilly and jumped off at the Haymarket.

I wasn't bothered about scoring, not only did the doctors pump me with mood altering drugs, but they also pumped me full of substance blocking drug, naltrexone.

I actually had no cravings it was some pretty good stuff.

Instead of hunting down crack, I went on a hunt for slasher. It was Christmas eve and this year, all I wanted for Christmas was to be slashers girl.

It wasn't too long before I found him on the corner of Endel Street. His eyes lit up as I walked towards him. He was on his push bike; it was kind of his getaway vechle.

I stopped in front of him and asked him what he wanted for Christmas. To which he replied "you".

I looked back and said to him, "well you have got me!". We went back to his hostel where I stayed for a few days.

We had to sneak me in and out though, because I wasn't supposed to be there. But it was the most magical few days of my life.

I was totally in love and felt like a princess. Listening intently as he showered me with soft words of affirmation.

The relationship, however, began with a rocky start, from our turbulent personality's but we finally got together properly after a brief stint of him being in prison.

Whilst Slasher was inside, I had got into a Look Ahead hostel in Bayswater, London. I was only in there a few days before Slasher was released. When he got out, he was so proud to call me his girl.

I was clean most day's but slasher and me would binge on crack at the weekends.

We had the most romantic summer that year, going on bike rides through Hyde park, having food by the duck pond. it was perfection.

After the honeymoon period though, crack became our number one priority and once again the addiction became more to me than life itself. Slasher and I were like bonnie and Clyde we got on so well one minute, in the blink of an eye we would be trying to kill each other.

There would be periods of time that we would be stuck to each other like glue, then other times it was like we were not even together.

I was with Slasher two years, then he became psychotic, trying to tie me up and strangle me or he would lock me in a flat, insisting he would kill me if I left him.

One day I was begging outside the Sainsbury's local on Tottenham Court Road, slasher hated it when I begged, and I knew word would get back to him that I was begging there.

Unfortunately for me, the police were also alerted that I was begging outside the store. Arrested on a warrant, I was remanded in custody and sent to Holloway prison. It wasn't my first time inside; it was my second.

The warrant was for a common assault on a community support officer. The officer had antagonized me whilst moving me on, so I spat on him. I was sentenced to six weeks in prison, which I would only serve three weeks of, as most charges are halved in time.

My second time in Holloway was more enlightening than the first time. The time before this one was for a begging charge; I was only in Holloway for the weekend and slept right through it. This time I was in for three weeks so I would say it was the most educational out of the two trips to the prison. Heading straight to the detox wing once the booking in process had finished, it felt more like a hospital ward. With cells ranging from four beds, two beds or single cells.

Sharing a cell was last on my list of priorities, there was no way! If only I had a choice. I was put in a four-bed cell with three other ladies. Two of the ladies were lovers and another was due to be released.

Don't get me wrong they were lovely ladies; I just couldn't handle the social interaction 24 hours a day. I thrived on isolation not integration.

The time went by quickly, and the next thing I knew I was released. Pleading that I would never be going to prison again, I found myself back in the middle of SoHo searching for Slasher, whom I hadn't heard from the past three weeks I had been inside. I was gutted to hear later that day that slasher too had been arrested and was now serving time in Pentonville Prison.

CHAPTER NINE – ROAD TO RECOVERY

Whilst slasher was inside for around ten weeks, I was chaotic. Staying awake for days on end smoking crack and cranking up my grafting methods. I had discovered clipping!

Clipping is where a guy thinks he's paying for sex, yet the girl takes the money and runs. Well, my young fresh face brought me many client's and lots of money. I would go days without stopping, I was in a world of my own.

Due to my extreme crack addiction, I would need some heroin to bring me back down, so it wasn't long before I was back on the gear again too…

I was sleeping rough in Piccadilly, London. I had been on a five-day crack binge and needed to stop and take a timeout. Crack was my only motivation, I had nothing to live for in the Groundhog Day that became my life. It was like I was lost in a world that I so desperately wanted to escape. A world that was driven by drugs and crime.

A life that is not worthy of human habitation.

On this night in particular I was bedding down outside the embassy opposite the Christopher Wren Church on Piccadilly.

I slept there a lot when I was on a comedown from the crack, it always felt much safer for some unknown reason. I had no blankets, so I huddled in a ball facing the door of the building.

I remember hearing a whisper it said "Kerri, come on I've chosen you" thinking I was hallucinating, I just ignored it. Feeling a little claustrophobic from being so close to the door, I turned, I opened my eyes in the restlessness and I saw what looked like a silhouette of a man sitting on the roof on the Cristopher Wren church. I was definitely tripping, right? I had been hammering the crack for days without even stopping for food.

No way, I was either dreaming or tripping there is absolutely no other explanation.

A few days later I was begging at the TSB cashpoint next door to the embassy, it was early in the evening and it had just turned dark.

Looking up to ask someone for change, I was shocked to see my boyfriend Slasher standing in front of me. He was fuming at me, he'd just been released from prison, where I abandoned him for my first love crack.

Now, he's here and I'm sat disrespecting him by begging. Boy did the proverbial hit the fan. After some harsh explicit language, and some saliva in my face, then off he went on his own mission of self-destruct.

Given the fact I had just got off lightly, in terms of Slashers wrath it was safe to say, my best bet now was to stay well away from Soho.

It must have been around 7pm because I remember thinking that it was about the time that the soup run goes to the strand.

Ever since I was thirteen, I have always found myself retreating to the Strand to where I spent most of my teenage years.

There would always be an elder there, someone who treated me like their little sister, or sometimes I'd have a street uncle.

It would be one of the older, longer standing homeless men, always a man though and often over-protective.

I guess thinking about it I just always needed a dominant male influence in my life. My daddy issues may also have a part to play in that too from a psychological perspective.

When I arrived at the strand there was already about three or four vans parked up.

One for food, one for clothes, one for blankets and sleeping bags, then there would be one for transporting the volunteers.

They were all religious people from different churches, doing their duty of goodwill, I liked the Irish gypsy's the best though, those are the ones I felt most drawn to.

Feeling pretty sorry for myself, I attempted to just get my soup, sandwich and blankets and then do one.

The gypsy's on the other hand wanted to stop and chat. Not really feeling the need for any idol chit chat, but ignorant I am not, so, I stopped to talk. The conversation, went a little something like this...

I highlight the word "Something like", please do not quote me on the actual conversation"

Gypsy Man 1: Hi, how are you, we haven't seen you in a while, you know you are welcome to come to our church, in Swanley.

Me: Yeah, I'm good thanks, erm yeah okay my best friend Ann lives in Swanley maybe next time I visit her.

Gypsy Man 1: Okay, well we have a minibus that comes to the car park at Charing Cross station, every Sunday to collect you guys so you are always welcome.

Me: Okay, thanks maybe I'll **stop** by one day.

Gypsy Man 2: Do you believe Kerri?

Me: Yeah, I believe in God

Gypsy Man 2: Do you believe in Jesus.

Me: I guess so He's the son of God, isn't he?

Gypsy Man 2: Yes, have you ever accepted Jesus Kerri?

Me: What do you mean?

Gypsy Man 2: Have you ever said a prayer inviting Jesus as your lord and savior?

Me: No!

Gypsy Man 2: Would you like to?

Me: Yeah okay… I guess I had nothing to lose.

Then the Gypsy Man asked me to repeat the words after him. They went a little something like this…

Dear God, I know that I am a sinner and there is nothing that I can do to save myself. I confess my complete helplessness to forgive my own sin or to work my way to heaven. At this moment I trust Christ alone as the One who bore my sin when He died on the cross. I believe that He did all that will ever be necessary for me to stand in your holy presence. I thank you that Christ was raised from the dead as a guarantee of my own resurrection. As best as I can, I now transfer my trust to Him. I am grateful that He has promised to receive me despite my many sins and failures. Father, I take you at your word. I thank you that I can face death now that you are my Savior. Thank you for the assurance that you will walk with me through the deep valley. Thank you for hearing this prayer. In Jesus' Name. Amen.

After declaring the prayer, I wrapped up the conversation to avoid any brain washing attempts and made a swift exit.

All filled up from my soup and sandwich, I made way back to Piccadilly to get my head down. I really couldn't be bothered with any drama, something that was inevitable if I stepped foot in Soho.

Not long after I sat down in my usual pitch at the Alliance and Leicester opposite Fortnum and Mason,

I got a twenty-pound drop and it burnt a hole straight through my blanket. The urge and temptation overcame the fear of bumping into Slasher. The next think I knew I was standing at the top of Wardour Street scoring two rocks.

Trying my best to go un-noticed I hurried to a secret smoking spot I used to go to. I had a secret space because I needed it.

I was so giving, even as a raging junky I was always giving my drugs away through lack of greed. I must have been the only person, to give a beggar my last pound to buy what they needed to get them through their pain. All in it together I used to say, ha, now I say sleep with one eye open in this world.

After my little session in my secret place across the other side of Oxford Street, I made way back to my pitch to call it a night. Having no idea just what had actually occurred. No idea of what door I had just opened.

I must have slept for sixteen hours solid because when I woke a whole day was missing, the day had already slipped away.

Instead of waking to commuters going to work, I was greeting them going home. Bonus! My cup was full, and I had made enough to score my first eye opener. Someone had kindly left some food too which I scoffed on the way to score.

It was around 5pm so it was rush hour, not just rush hour for workers but also rush hour for scoring too. There were shotters but they were scarce, avoiding getting "Rushed" by the police. The only thing is, when dealers go into hiding there ends up being a big huddle of drug addicts in the middle of Shaftsbury avenue desperate to score.

This day in particular, one of those desperate drug addicts was slasher. He had been on a proper blowout since his release from prison and was strung out for a pipe.

As soon as he saw me it was like a red flag to the bull. He made his way towards me, to what I thought was a reconciliation maybe, turned into me getting sparked right in the mouth which led to an instant fat lip, then off he rode on his bike down the middle of China Town.

He must have done a left on to Shaftsbury Avenue because he was back within minutes. The shotter had just turned up as he hit me, so he did a circle around the block, picked up his crack and disappeared.

Scurrying off in the opposite direction, I made way to the back of Jermyn Street in Piccadilly to smoke the drugs I had just purchased.

Days past and weeks too, all in which time I grew tired of the hamster wheel I was living on. Slasher and I were hanging on by a thread, there was no value to our lives let alone relationship.

One night, sitting crouched on the floor outside the embassy, feeling defeated and depressed, I Looked up at the church in front of me and began to sob uncontrollably.

I cried and cried till I couldn't cry anymore, pleading "if God was real, why am I living this way" going on to say, "God if you are real get me out of this now!"

I had hit rock bottom, I needed out. Surely there was no more this life could throw at me. I was twenty-three with no life ahead of me, surely this wasn't my destiny. Was it?

After that night, I began to feel stronger, more able to bounce back from whatever was upsetting me from the night before. Allowing my inner strength to surface I began mentally equipping myself for the fight.

With this new-found determination I was able to think more clearly, find logic within my current circumstance, the sort of logic as to why am I here exactly? With this thought in mind, I decided it was time to get off of the streets.

Withdrawing from heroin, I made way to Look Ahead Bayswater, a hostel I stayed in previously.

I had been evicted because, I threw a tantrum and called one of the lady staff a female dog. I had an argument with Slasher, and it got heated, when the staff member tried to intervene, I told her where to go which ended in my eviction. It didn't help my case that she was the manager of the project.

Here I was though, making my way there, not quite sure what was going to happen when I got there. I knew you had to be referred in but that did not stop me.

When I first arrived, I asked to see the lady who I thought was the manager, to be informed that she was no longer there. I asked if I could see the new manager instead, to my joy it was Tom, someone who I got on quite well with in L.A Bayswater.

Tom called me into his office and informed me that I knew the process of referrals. Pleading with him that I just wanted help, and it was too long going through the process of representing at a day center first to then get referred into the next available hostel. It wasn't long before Tom responded with "let me see what I can do".

Within a couple of hours, I was moved back in, somehow, I had found favor and fortunately for me my old room was empty.

L.A Bayswater is actually the nicest homeliest hostel I ever lived in. It had more of a children's home feel to it. The staff there were so supportive, they would attend every appointment with you in the rehabilitation process. I was ready to take advantage of every aspect of that service.

I had no belongings with me, just a chicken and mushroom pot noodle that I had robbed from the Tesco on Bayswater road. I had no intention of using, I wanted out!

I withdrew from heroin for the next twenty-four hours, cold turkey. It was the worst sickness I have ever been subject to. Cold sweats, hot flushes, stomach cramps and restlessness and so on.

I spent the whole night in the tv room watching movies on Sky.

I attended the doctor's the next day and was referred to S.R.A.C. A drug dependency clinic run by the NHS. I was prescribed methadone and allocated a keyworker through the rehabilitation center the Hungerford Drug Project.

One week past, then another week, the methadone kicked in properly and I was rearing for clean life. I felt so in control of my life, for the first time ever, I was dreaming of a better life.

Slasher was in prison again and we weren't talking, in fact I had completely forgotten about him in terms of any romance or emotional attachment.

No! Nothing could hold me back now! Not one thing.

CHAPTER TEN – LIVE OR DIE

Feeling fresh and looking for purpose, I started to attend the Hungerford Drug Project drop-in on Wardour Street.

Okay, Wardour Street is kind of shotters galore, but I was determined, and this was a huge test to that determination. I was not backing down.

There would be all sorts of services available to make you feel more human and opportunities to enhance your learning.

Some days there would be I.T training or photography, my favorite was sound engineering. There would always be lunch club followed with some kind of alternative therapy.

Acupuncture was the one I found the most beneficial, it would relax me into a space of complete serenity. I would become so relaxed; it would put me to sleep.

Part of the service was a blood Bourne virus clinic, Fiona from S.R.A.C would come in every Wednesday to do blood testing for intravenous related virus's such as Hepatitis and HIV.

With nothing to lose, I decided to get tested.

Within a week of being tested, I was called in to Fiona's office, where she gave me a full house on the diagnosis's.

I'd caught all three! What had I done, I had signed my own death warrant with my chaotic behavior, this was something that could not be fixed?

Completely distraught at the consequences of my own action's there was only one thing that could ease my pain, I needed a pipe and I needed it quick.

I had so many thoughts in my head, screaming what have you done, what are you going to tell Slasher? You have to tell him; he could have it too!

The only thing that was going to shut up the voices was a big fat pipe.

One pipe turned in to two, then three and then the next thing I knew I was on a four-day bender. Then when I was finally ready to face the music, I went back to the hostel. Only to find out that Slasher had been looking for me. What?! Slasher is out?

Yes, slasher was out and on the war path again because I had once again abandoned him while he was inside. I really didn't need his selfish insecurities right now. I just made way to my bedroom to bed.

A couple of hours later I was called by the staff, Slasher was at the door and I needed to sign him in, really!!? What did he want?

I guessed that this would be the perfect opportunity to tell him. Blaming it on a sexual assault that took place the last time I lived in the hostel, it was brushed under the carpet as a not my fault kind of issue.

It was my fault though wasn't it. I was a dirty little smack head, and this was my own doing.

I use the term smack head because that was the label society gave me, not because it is how I look at homeless people. Or myself anymore!

Inevitably, this was a massive set back in my recovery, I was going to die, I was a ticking time bomb, my life as I knew it was over.

This was the nail to the coffin for sure. So much for making a clean break! This life had to have some kind of vendetta against me.

Smoking continuously again I lost all control; it was a live or die mentality…

With this new revelation, came hurricane Kerri! I was a whirlwind of emotion and Slasher was Jekyll and Hyde, blowing hot and cold from one minute to the next.

I got into trouble at look ahead Bayswater, so, I was moved into the last chance saloon of hostels. Look Ahead Victoria.

L.A Victoria was one of the most notorious hostels in Westminster it was more like a legalized crack den. If you wanted any gear, you just had to rock up at Look Ahead Victoria, and you would be sorted.

Recovery in a place like this hostel was not going to be done easily.

It had been around six weeks since my diagnosis and I was growing tired of the constant crack binging. I was body popping for five days solid, dropping for twenty-four hours, to then get up to do it all again.

Something within me, so desperately wanted to change, but for what? What did I have that was worth fighting for?

Then one day, clear as a bell, I heard a voice in my head, I heard these words…

"If you don't get your act together, you will be dead in two years and will never see Jack again"

It was so distinct, so powerful!

Once again, I would try recovery, I can so do this, I thought to myself. Slasher and I were evidently over, we were hanging on to each other by a thread, but it was over.

I was living in the women's block of the hostel; and I'd just started to settle in and take advantage of the rehabilitation services they offered.

I was looking forward to doing the military fitness in particular, because apparently fitness is good for drug recovery as it releases the same endorphins as crack does.

The more of a routine I got into, the more relaxed I became. Part of that routine would be having one can of tenants super to get me to sleep at night.

One can is enough to fuel a rocket, it's lethal. I only needed the one though to get me off to sleep at night.

Returning from the shop one day, I was sat on the steps outside of the hostel, just chatting to some friends who lived there also.

Along came a woman, who I never really got on with. I really didn't need any drama! However, drama was her middle name.

She started to goad me and really wind me up.

Back then my fuse was short so before I knew it, we were in fisty cuffs on the middle of the street outside the hostel.

When provoked I would become extremely violent! Not the bitchy, hair pulling and scratching type of violent.

No, I would fight like one of us is dying in the fight and it isn't going to be me! So, its safe to say I didn't hold back. Finally, staff came and separated us.

Returning to my room happily, my ritual of tenants super, book and bed was already past due.

Just as I was settling into bed, there was a loud banging on my door, I jumped up, bricking it. as I reached for my trackys to put on, as I was in my night clothes. The next thing I knew I was being pinned down by at least five police officers, arrested and brutally bundled into the back of a police van.

What the fudge was going on? Why was I the one being arrested? She started the fight!

Later on, during the interview, the police questioned me about a bite mark on the woman's hand. I laughed at the allegation because in my eyes she was the dog not me.

I didn't bite anyone! She was lying! After the interview I was charged with serious assault. I was lucky that it wasn't attempted murder given my HIV status, I was mortified!

Due to this ridiculous event, I was forced to leave the hostel immediately, so, with no fixed abode I was held in custody till the Monday morning, when the court would decide my fate.

Luckily for me there were staff working on my behalf in the Look Ahead hostel, they managed to get me into Dean Street Hostel. A residence not even fit for humanity.

It was almost immediately after the moment I moved into the hostel at Dean Street that I was ready to score.

What was the point! Every time I tried to break away something just held me back. If this wasn't a sign of the life, I'm destined to live then what was it?

So, jumping back onto the hamster wheel I became reliant on my old friend crack again. And something really strange happened…

One morning just as the sun was coming up, I was smoking in the alley way opposite the Hungerford Project, when Slasher had announced to all the cats (smokers) that I was HIV, trying to cause trouble.

It was like they scurried away from me like I was going to give it to them, just by touch. There was a black guy that I had never seen before there and he said to me to go with him for a minute, when I walked with him, he said these words…

"It's Okay! You will be healed of HIV just believe "

He prayed over me and then just disappeared down Shaftsbury Avenue towards Piccadilly, never to be seen again.

It was a strange encounter, one which I didn't truly understand. How could this man be so bold, to suggest that one day I'm going to be free of HIV!

I just gave up, admitting defeat I was back on it!

With that live or die mentality, the latter being my number one goal. With no regard to life in general, it had not even entered my mind that I was supposed to appear in court for the serious assault charge that the woman in the hostel, falsely accused me of.

So, it wasn't too long before I found myself being transported in the back of a sweat box, to Holloway prison, on a warrant for failing to surrender.

Due to failing to appear meant another charge added to my case. There's no way I was getting out unless I was released on a not guilty.

Straight to detox I went, reuniting with friends from the street, friends that would get them self nicked in the winter to find refuge and retreat from the cold nights.

We used to call it a holiday to Holloway. About two days after my imprisonment to my complete joy, I discovered that the very same woman that got me nicked, had been put into the cell opposite me.

Oh, how I wanted to make her life hell! Everyone on the wing was going to know that this little female dog had got me arrested. Not to mention for false allegations too!

The thing is, within about a week we became friends, then not long after I was moved to the main prison and never saw her again.

It had been around a month that I had been inside there was no sign of me getting out either. Then, one morning about five-thirty in the morning.

A screw came and called me for court, to begin with I thought I was dreaming so continued sleeping. Then she returned, to which point I jumped up and got dressed.

Slightly confused as I had no court date, I plodded down to the foyer anyway to begin the signing out process.

Strip search at six in the morning, every woman's dream! After a very long day in court I was released without charge. Somebody in the hostel came forward and testified that she actually bit herself, so, I was released with no further action.

Having been clean for the best part of five weeks, I was completely focused. I wasn't going back to the crack and the drama that followed it.

No! I was taking a stand this time.

I stood in a phone box typed in the Newcastle dialing code, followed with my Aunties telephone number...

After a few rings, she picked up the phone. "Can I come to yours" I asked her, she replied with "of course you can!"

So off I went, back to the place where my life began.

I was twenty-four years old and had the weight of the world on my shoulders, but off I went to Newcastle. Leaving that messed up life once and for all.

CHAPTER ELEVEN – FINALLY FREE

Back in Newcastle, and fighting strong, I began the full recovery process. I knew no dealers in the area and crack was alien in the northeast, well, decent crack anyway.

Temptation was nowhere to be seen. Whilst I was in prison I was on a small dose of methadone, something like 30ml, I was only prescribed it inside because it's the hardest thing to detox from.

When I returned to the north east, I chose not to engage with the drug services because I decided to go cold turkey from the methadone.

After around six weeks the worst of it was over. I was officially clean! My life was my own again, it was amazing. I loved living at my aunties house, but my cousins can be quite nasty with their tongues without realizing how nasty they sound at times.

With my insecurities after around five months in October 2008 I left Newcastle once again and headed straight to the west end.

Although yes, I did go and score as soon as I landed in Soho, I only used for a few days.

I then found myself extremely ill from a severe chest infection in the lobby of Look Ahead Victoria, begging them to take me back in.

I somehow found favor with a couple of ladies that worked in L.A Victoria. Kath and Lucy were two in particular. They bent over backwards to get me back into the hostel and succeeded.

I moved in around October which is when I met the next love of my life. He won't appreciate me mentioning his name, so I'll call him "My Ex!"

My Ex had the gift of the gab, he could charm the birds out of the trees. That's how he got me, his charm! At first, I played hard to get, but as the weeks past we drew closer, until only one thing stood in the way of moving any further.

That thing being my health status.

I hadn't really had the conversation before, how would it go?...

Hey, let's sleep together, oh before we do, I have HIV?...

I was terrified to tell him. But after some Dutch courage, I finally plucked up the nerve to have the conversation with him. Only to be told he already knew because someone in the hostel already told him.

Then the next thing we knew the deed was done. Then a matter of weeks later I found out I was pregnant with his baby.

It was just after Christmas when I found out. Happy and ready to be a mum for real this time, I was prepared to do it all on my own.

Let's face it the relationship was barely three months old, now there's a pregnancy.

When I told My Ex, his emotions were varied, and it took a couple of days for the news to sink in.
A few weeks passed, and it was valentines day. I was six weeks pregnant, and vomiting blood.

Okay, I can't miss this out, I had gone up west on a 24hr binge, all because social services were getting involved to do a risk assessment.

Well, instead of being sensible and behaving myself, I went into complete meltdown mode and went on a binge.

Which resulted in me being checked into A&E with blood in my vomit.

The vomiting was scraping the back of my throat which caused my throat to bleed, so, the doctor prescribed me with some sickness medication and told me I could go home after a quick scan.

My Ex had come to the hospital, but I told him to jog on because he was stressing me out. Just after I got rid of My Ex, I was called in for my scan.

As I lay there with the cold jelly on my tummy, the sonographer turned to ask me if I knew I was having twins?...

I just burst out crying with joy, TWINS!!

I was the first one in my family to have twins after my nana had hers. I had two for the price of one, I now had a chance to make up for what I lost with Jack.

When I told My Ex, he was really angry because he already knew because of, me and my big mouth! I had told the whole hostel before I told him.

To be fair he was nowhere to be found, and my excitement got the better of me.

Due to my current circumstances I was moved into the cluster flats, the independent living part of the hostel, where I was to stay until I was seven months gone. I was fortunate to have Kat and Lucy as my keyworkers and Leah as my drug worker, the dream team as I call them.

With their help I stayed focused and kept my eye on the ball. Attending every appointment and assessment the social workers expected me to attend.

When I was seven months gone, I had to move on from Look Ahead due to safety reasons.

It was not safe for a heavily pregnant lady to be staying there and the hostel could not risk having me there. So, me and My Ex moved into a temporary B&B just by Marble Arch where we stayed until the 18th August 2009, which was when we moved into our two bedrooms flat in Churchill Gardens, Pimlico.

Look Ahead Victoria closed later that summer and remains empty to this day! 150+ rooms sat empty and derelict. Just felt I needed to add that.

Two weeks after we moved into the flat, I was booked in for a c-section.

On Tuesday 1st September at 2:59pm Charlie George was born weighing 5lb2oz. Then one minute later his Sister Rebecca Christine joined him weighing 5lb5oz.

As My Ex held Charlie, the nurse handed me Rebecca, I just looked into her eyes, feeling content and complete. I was a mother and this time I was going to get to be a mum too.

I had jumped through every hoop during pregnancy, so, there was no reason the twins couldn't come home.

A week after the birth, after some intensive tests and monitoring we were discharged from hospital, time to take my babies home. A day I longed for, since giving birth to my firstborn Jack.

My Ex and I were besotted when we had the twins, we had a fiery relationship from the get-go but when we became parents it brought us closer together.

However, my insecurities would always rear their ugly head and make an appearance within the stress of being sleep deprived. Eventually this impacted the relationship in a negative way.

CHAPTER TWELVE – THE HEALING BEGINS

It was early November 2009 I had not long given birth to the twins. Due to my health status I was unable to give birth naturally in case one of the babies contracted the illness through delivery.

Along with that precaution, there had to be regular blood tests to monitor my levels of the HIV virus and also to make sure that the twins were all clear.

Which they were to our relief!

When I asked the nurse about Hepatitis, she informed me they didn't have that either, neither did I!

I looked at her in shock and asked her if she was sure, to which she responded with yes, she was sure and that the only explanation is, that I have the antibodies in my blood, the antibodies must have fought and cured the virus.

Okay, so I had to get this straight I didn't have Hepatitis just HIV. No plausible explanation I was just cured.

"Hep B can be cured by antibodies, but Hep C, can't! Only medication can cure the latter.

Not really grasping the fact that I had been cured of an illness that is only curable by taking a drug for twelve months called interferon, yet I'm cured without it.

So, this was it, perfection! Neither of the twins had contracted any virus and I was cured too! This had to be a miracle, right?...

Due to my instability as a young adult I was watched like a hawk by social services but after bending over backwards and proving my ability to parent, Social services discharged the case after six months.

A day of complete victory for me and Leah my drug worker. She came with me to court. It was one of the best days of my life.

The judge said I deserved a pat on the back, for the complete reversal of ways since my battle with the local authority over Jack.

Proud was an understatement.

The first two years of mine and my ex's relationship were fine, we argued but we always made up quickly.

Then one day in February 2012 My Ex decided he didn't want me anymore and cheated on me, he just disappeared for days on end to go and be with a different woman.

I found out quite quickly, I'm not stupid I knew he had cheated, where else would he have been!

I left him the day I found out, taking the kids to my aunties house in Newcastle.

I feel like I need to clarify, my relationship with the twins dad was rarely a good one, and we remain amicable now for the sake of the twins, I have tried to avoid going into too much detail of my time with this man.

For my own reasons. I would rather just skim past the three years I was with him.

In Newcastle I was fast tracked through the housing and on the waiting list for a house.

While I was there, I hit rock bottom, completely broken from the recent events. I turned to a different drug, this time I started hammering the speed.

Along with the speed I was drinking loads, I just didn't care. Not long after social services were once again involved.

My chaotic behavior was resulting in me getting myself noticed by the authorities! I had to get my act together. Days before the twins third birthday, I decided to return to my flat in Pimlico, thinking it would shake social services, instead it made me look even more unstable.

The thing is not only had I moved my children back to the center of an abusive relationship, I had also informed the police and the authorities that My Ex was an abusive partner whilst I was still in a place of anger.

Which made things extremely difficult when I tried to allow him to see the children. Social services provided me with a no contact order. My Ex was not allowed near the children.

When I returned, I was fooled by an illusion that My Ex and I could rekindle our love and be a happy family again, My Ex on the other hand thought he could play me and his mistress at the same time.

I knew he was with her, yet he was living in my house, sleeping in my bed, I began to find solace at the bottom of the bottle, letting thoughts of them together mess with my head.

The past twelve months had been hard, my twins dad had cheated on me and it was time for a clean break.

I had two choices I could either move to Tooting where my best friend Tasha lived, or I could move to Wallasey for a complete fresh start.

The decision was a tough one because I would have loved to have been closer to Tasha, but the logical decision was to move to Wallasey. Once the decision was made the house hunting began.

I wasn't sure how I was going to pay for the move, being on benefits I knew where to look for help. I applied for a community care grant and budgeting loan through the social fund department of the social security office.

Once the forms are received, you can get a decision within six weeks. I applied for both expecting a knock back on at least one.

Whilst I waited for my answer by post, I searched online for possible houses to rent, quickly becoming deflated at needing a deposit and a month's rent upfront.

I wasn't giving up! So, I then decided to have a look on the Westminster.gov website to see what help I could get.

To my surprise, I stumbled across a section that mentioned a private landlord scheme, that went on to say that if you relinquish your tenancy with the Westminster council and go private in another area, the council will pay you to hand in your keys.

The price they pay varies, depending on whether or not you are in temporary or permanent housing if you live in a permanent house or flat you get £10,000 but if you live in a temporary accommodation you can get £3000 provided you didn't have any rent arrears.

"Kerching!"

I was only in a temporary flat so was only given three grand, but it was more than enough to get me started in Wallasey.

I found a three-bedroom house pretty quickly and Sandy viewed it for me and accepted immediately. I was ready to go I just needed to borrow the money until mine came through, to put up front for the new house and I was set.

A day or two after the tenancy was agreed I received two brown envelopes in the post, I knew what they were before I opened them, I opened them in a hurry to see what they said.

To my complete surprise I had been awarded £600 budgeting loan and a £900 community care grant.

Winner, winner chicken dinner! That was a total of four and a half grand to move up to Wallasey, all handed to me without stress, there had to be a mix up in the universe somewhere, these sort of good things don't usually happen to people like me.

CHAPTER THIRTEEN – MOVING ON

The day of the move ran smoothly, although we got caught on the train with a load of football fans trying to get to the match.

We arrived safely at our new home around 2pm. I remember feeling like it was the most content feeling I had felt since giving birth. A brand-new start for me and my little cherubs!

Not only had we stepped into a brand-new life, but we had stepped into a proper family too.

The children's great auntie was very eager to take the twins to Sunday school every week, I was quite happy to have a break so I would stay at home and chill while they were gone.

I would insist that I do believe in God, but I don't do church. What was the point of going to some middle-class service, to be looked upon as some dirty little ex junkie?

No way was I opening myself up to that judgement. If only I knew then what I know now.

My life seemed so perfect, everything just felt like it was meant to be. I now had a supportive family that were encouraging me to make better choices.

I had a determination to be the best mum I could be to my children, there was nothing that could lead me back to that darkness now.

Trouble is, loneliness started to creep in, and I began to feel home sick, which made me resent my new family in Wallasey for suggesting the idea of me moving there.

They had done absolutely nothing wrong I just became extremely insecure.

Whenever I start getting close to anyone, I instantly feel like I must sever all ties before I get hurt. So, I began to lash out for no reason causing negativity within the family unit. Upsetting everyone around me.

Then one day everything changed, I was invited on a day out with the children's church, a non-religious fun day in a park in Warrington.

I accepted because it did sound fun and the twins would enjoy it. There were two double decker busses filled with people that were all attending this church day out.

As I chatted to the lady in front of me, I realized that actually, these Christian folk are not really that judgmental after all. In fact, they seem very accepting and inviting.

I can't deny this really put me at ease about the whole churchy thing.

A few weeks passed from the big church day out and the children were continuously attending every Sunday, as I chilled at home enjoying the break.

It was then September…

Every year the church has a gift giving service for all of the children and young people that attend the Sunday school. Well the twins were too going to receive a gift.

They were only four at the time, but I would never miss anything like that, it was like a little school assembly where they were called to the front for a little gift from the church, which is usually a bible or story book.

So, there I was sitting in the back row of this little family church in Wallasey, completely out of my depth when,

Charlie walks up to me and asks if I can come to church every week…

Erm…. What do you say to your four-year-old when he asks that kind of question?...

"We'll See"

Apparently, it was not up to me though!

Every week from that day on, I felt a deep urge within me to get ready on Sunday morning and attend church with the children.

I actually enjoyed it!! The songs and the story's from the Bible had me fixated every week; I was so hungry for more. As the months past the more I felt myself changing as a person.

Like the old me was slipping away and a new me was surfacing. From that first time in September, through to the following April, I grew deeper into the whole church thing.

On the last Sunday of April just days before my 30TH birthday I declared my love for Jesus and was baptized in water.

A feeling so immense, one that I could never forget. I was a new creation, washed clean in the water. The old had left me as the new became rooted.

The coming months were turbulent to say the least. I was doing everything within me to stay on this new path of faith.

I obtained a voluntary position at a Christian youth work service, with the drug and alcohol awareness team. I was part of the worship band at church and attending every service and small group I could cram in.

I loved this brand-new life. Nothing could ever take this joy from me. I was happy and content with all that I had.

Over time though cracks appeared, as they always do when I get settled for any long period of time. I had become very close to a group of the ladies from the church, a little too close maybe.

In September 2015, precisely two years into my conversion, I had fallen out with the group of ladies. It was a bad argument that even now the relationships have never fully recovered.

There was a big church weekend away to MCYC in Wales. It was something the church does every other year to build on the fellowship of the church.

This year someone had very kindly paid for the children and I to attend the weekend away. It had been done anonymously as a blessing.

Even to this day, I'm totally blown away by the generosity of that person! That weekend, changed my life forever...

CHAPTER FOURTEEN – I AM CHANGED

The weekend was catered to bring us together as a church. There was a guest speaker who would bring us a message over the course of the weekend.

I remember feeling awkward anyway because I was surrounded by the ladies who I had recently fell out with. Then the Pastor guy starts his sermon for the weekend, based on the book of Romans.

By the time the weekend was over I was in pieces, completely distraught by all of my wrong doings in the past. All of my sins and failures washing over me, making me feel completely unworthy of God's love.

I ran to my chalet toilet and locked the door, where I began to sob uncontrollably. How can God love me, after all I have done?

How can He forgive me when I hold so much of a grudge for the ladies across the green, outside the chalets?

I heard a knock on the bathroom door, it was Liz. She was asking if I was okay… No, I said as I sobbed through the door.

I was on my knees heartbroken and I had no idea why.

Liz and I spoke for the whole journey home, it took around two hours. I can't quite remember what we spoke about, but it brought me peace and clarity.

Later that night, I felt compelled to put my favorite worship song on, so I did…

WOW!! I must have looked like a raving lunatic, dancing round my living room singing "Praise the Lord" "Thank You Jesus"

It was as if I was possessed or something…

After this brief encounter, I felt the need to share my experience, so, I messaged my friend Claire.

Completely away with the fairy's I typed out what had just happened, starting with "Claire I think I have just been saved" I remember I was shaking whilst I waited on her reply.

"You already are saved" The reply came through... "You have just been spiritually saved" Huh? ...

So, it may seem that I had encountered the Holy Spirit in a spiritual baptism, something I had no clue about.

My life transformed from this moment on, a 360-degree turn, that could have only ever have been made possible, by the hand of God.

As I look back in my life, I can't count the amount of times that God has showed up, trying to bring me back on to a path of righteousness.

There is so much more to my story and I could go on forever, but this installment is at it's end now.

Please keep a lookout for the next installment of this story, one that is filled with magnificent testimonies of the Love that I have encountered since I encountered the Holy Spirit.

THE END

46191171R00098

Printed in Poland
by Amazon Fulfillment
Poland Sp. z o.o., Wrocław